Rise Above
And
Own Your Power

A GUIDE TO RECLAIM INNER STRENGTH, CONFIDENCE AND SELF-WORTH

By

LIZAIDA ALVAREZ

Rise Above and Own Your Power

Copyright © 2024 Lizaida Alvarez

All Rights Reserved.

ISBN: 979-8-9896259-1-8

All rights reserved. No part of this book be reproduced or transmitted in any form, or by any information storage and retrieval system, without permission in writing by the author.

All translations of this work must be approved in writing by the author. Please contact Lizaida Alvarez for permission to translate and distribution agreements.

LizaidaAlvarez.com

ABOUT THE LOTUS FLOWER

Lotus flower is a symbol that represents inner strength, confidence, and self-worth. The lotus is often associated with personal growth and transformation, as it emerges from murky waters to loom into a beautiful flower. It symbolizes strength and resilience in the face of adversity, as well as the ability to rise above challenges and find inner peace. The lotus also represents self-worth and confidence, as it stands tall and proud despite its humble beginnings. Its elegant and captivating.

DEDICATION

My dearest mother Carmen,

Your resilience in facing every difficulty and challenge throughout your life has inspired, guided my entire existence, and instilled an immense sense of resilience that I carry with me every day.

Though your childhood may have been difficult, you have emerged as an exceptional individual, compassionate toward those in need, and selfless in your empathy, willing to sacrifice on behalf of others, molding me into who I am today. I will forever appreciate and remember your positive influence, as it helped shape into who I am today. I will always be thankful.

As I travel my own path through life, it gives me comfort knowing you are by my side. Thank you for everything you've done to support my well-being. From all the sacrifices to showing me unconditional love, I truly am blessed that we share such an intimate bond, and I will always treasure having you here by my side.

My beloved children, Brianna, Carlos, and Xavier,

This book I dedicate to you, my most valued inspirations in life. As your mother, my priority is setting an excellent example and helping break generational cycles. My hope for you is that you know you can achieve anything you put your mind to. I will always remind you of your inner strength, confidence, and worthiness.

My hope for this book is to offer you strategies and techniques that serve as a road map when you are facing life's obstacles. Know that you deserve love, respect, happiness, and all the good things life has to offer. You have it in you to overcome negative self-talk and create a positive self-image.

Remember that setbacks and challenges are part of life's journey; each step you take brings you closer to reaching your ultimate goal. I believe in you and I am proud of the incredible individuals you are becoming!

Dear reader,

Thank you so much for taking the time to read my words. Your support means more than I could ever express. My hope is that my words provide strength as you navigate life's obstacles.

My goal is that my story provides inspiration and motivation to overcome any hurdles or difficulties you encounter. While life may present us with obstacles and we may feel helpless or discouraged, know that every obstacle can be overcome with perseverance, patience, and an optimistic mindset.

No matter your struggles—be they personal, career-related, or any other form—let me remind you that no matter the challenge you can overcome it. Learn from both my story as well as from personal experience to strengthen your determination and keep moving forward!

Please accept my sincerest appreciation and thanks for allowing me to share my words. I wish you well on your journey and hope that you continue finding encouragement and motivation along the way.

Table of Contents

INTRODUCTION 10

Chapter 1
CLAMING YOUR POWER 13

Chapter 2
SELF-DOUBT 27

Chapter 3
LIMITING BELIEFS 41

Chapter 4
INNER STRENGTH 60

Chapter 5
CONFIDENCE 78

Chapter 6
NAVIGATING OBSTACLES 96

Chapter 7
USING YOUR VOICE..110

Chapter 8
STRONG RELATIONSHIPS...127

Chapter 9
PASSION AND PURPOSE..146

Chapter 10
REFLECTIONS ON THE JOURNEY................................... 165

ACKNOWLEDGMENTS 178

ABOUT THE AUTHOR 180

INTRODUCTION

We face a world that often tries to break us down, whether through society's expectations, criticism, or personal struggles. It can be easy to feel powerless and uncertain of one's self-worth. But the truth is we all possess inner strengths, confidence, and self-worth that we can draw on when faced with difficulties or goals that seem out of reach.

Rise Above and Own Your Power is an inspirational guide designed to help individuals reclaim their inner strength, confidence, and self-worth. Through relatable stories, insightful advice, and practical tips from Lizaida Alvarez's book, readers will learn to overcome self-doubt, release themselves from limiting beliefs, and step into their power. Through this book she hopes readers can navigate life's obstacles and emerge stronger, more resilient, and more confident than ever before.

In this book, we will explore the challenges individuals in modern society face, and how these difficulties may impair our sense of self-worth and confidence. We will look at sources of self-doubt and limiting beliefs as well as strategies for overcoming them. Furthermore, we will discover ways to build inner strength, cultivate confidence, and find our voice within an often-intolerant world.

This book is for anyone who wishes to reclaim their power and live an inspiring, meaningful, and fulfilling life. To address personal challenges to professional goals, *Rise Above and Own Your Power* is an indispensable resource that will guide you to overcome life's hurdles more successfully and emerge stronger, more resilient, and more confident than ever before.

So, if you're ready to take charge and regain your power, let's get to work.

CHAPTER

one

CLAMING YOUR POWER

Chapter 1
CLAIMING YOUR POWER

It had been a year since my breakup from my husband of 20 years, and I was still struggling to pick up the pieces of my shattered life. For so long, I had defined myself by my role as a wife and mother. But now that I was on my own, I realized that I had lost touch with who I was as an individual.

As I navigated a difficult divorce, I felt a sense of despair wash over me. I couldn't shake the feeling that I had failed, that I wasn't good enough. It was as if my entire sense of self-worth was tied to the success or failure of my relationship. I felt lost and struggled to find meaning in my life without my partner, and the thought of starting over was daunting, but I refused to give up. I knew that there was more to life and I had to reclaim my inner strength, confidence, and self-worth. As time passed and I began to heal, I realized that my worth as a person was not defined by my relationship status.

I began prioritizing myself by engaging in activities that brought me joy or had been on my bucket list but I had not found the courage or time to pursue. For example, visiting the park often, going for nature walks or simply sitting alone to reflect and write became part of my routine. Feeling lost and not knowing where I was going, I flew back home to reconnect with my roots and reconnect with my younger self who reminded me where I'm headed. Since returning, I have pursued real estate sales, begun networking, met so many incredible people whom I now consider friends, went to a shooting range for the first time (intimidating but exhilarating experience!), manifested my first girls' trip, and even sighed up for salsa dance lessons. With each new experience, I felt a little more confidence.

Of course, my journey was not easy, and I encountered many challenges along the way. These included financial strain due to divorce proceedings, dating challenges, and learning how to be a single parent to my three children. But I refused to let these obstacles hold me back; instead, they only made me stronger!

As I continued my journey of self-discovery, I began to see the world in a new light. I realized that challenges faced by individuals were real but not unbeatable. While society often tries to tear people down, I also felt the incredible resilience and strength that individuals possess. It became clear to me that we have the capacity to overcome adversity and achieve great things.

Through it all, I discovered my worth was not defined by marital status or career alone. It came from within myself, and once I reclaimed my inner strength, confidence, and sense of self-worth, life became richer and more rewarding than I could ever have anticipated. I learned to find happiness within myself and appreciate all aspects of life that brought me joy, though this journey wasn't always smooth sailing. In the end it led me toward greater self-awareness and personal growth.

CLAIMING YOUR POWER IN A WORLD THAT TRIES TO TEAR YOU DOWN

I remember when someone suggested that I should return to Puerto Rico, where I'm from, and learn English. At that time, I was self-conscious about my English-speaking skills, and this comment has only made me feel more inadequate. It was as if this person was saying I did not belong in America, that I was somehow less than because English was not my first language. I refused to let their words bring me down. Instead, I used them as motivation to work harder. I focused on improving my English-speaking skills, and I pursued my dreams with a new sense of determination.

From humble beginnings, I've always been curious and open-minded. I enjoy learning new things and strive for the future with anticipation and optimism. Because of this, people told me I wanted a life I couldn't live—like I was dreaming too big and should be more realistic. Knowing it was the projection of their insecurity and limitations speaking through those words, I used them as fuel to create my life the way I wanted. Refusing to let anyone tell me I couldn't do something made my determination stronger than ever!

Rise Above and Own Your Power

The day I knew my marriage was going to end in divorce. It was a sunny day, but all I felt was darkness. The end of my marriage left me feeling broken and lost. I had given so much of myself to my relationship that I didn't know who I was without it. I felt like I had lost my power, my strength, my confidence, and my sense of self.

As if this dark process wasn't hard enough, I was told some very hurtful words such as, "You aren't going to amount to anything," "You won't ever be anybody," "You are going to end up in the ghetto" and "You won't be able to survive without your spouse." These words were like a knife to my heart, they cut deep and left me feeling small and insignificant.

As I doubted myself and my abilities, I began to question their words about me and wonder if I was asking too much or trying for too much in life. But then something clicked, as I knew that those words didn't fully represent who I am, knowing that their words had no power over me except if I allowed it. After all, I am strong, wise, and capable, so I refused to let anyone tear me down!

As soon as I set my mind to something, I started working harder than ever before, pursuing my dreams with a newfound determination. And slowly but surely, I began to see the fruits of my labor. I accomplished things that I never thought were possible, and I felt a sense of pride and confidence that I had never felt before!

Reclaiming my power wasn't an easy journey, but it was well worth it. Through this experience I discovered that I am far stronger and more resilient than expected and my sense of worth comes from within, not from others' opinions of me. Regaining my power allowed me to live life on my terms, pursue my dreams and be my best self. I am proud of who I am and where I come from. I'm not going to let others define who I am or what my value is.

I'm thankful for every negative word spoken toward me; these hurtful remarks were the fuel that I needed to reclaim my power and become the best version of myself.

Reclaiming your power in an environment that seeks to diminish you can be both a challenging and empowering process. Doing so requires acknowledging any conditioning that has led you to believe you don't have what it takes to be successful, that you are not enough, that you do not have the skills or abilities to succeed, or that you are somehow less valuable than others.

To regain your power, it is necessary to acknowledge that these beliefs are false. You have the strength within yourself to overcome any obstacle and reach your goals regardless of what others think or say about you. Doing this requires inner work such as practicing self-compassion and self-love while building self-confidence and challenging negative self-talk.

An effective way to reclaim your power is finding and using your voice to advocate for yourself in personal and professional relationships, while speaking out against injustice or inequality in society at large. Another key element of taking back control lies in taking concrete steps toward your goals.

Claiming Your Power is about acknowledging and accepting your inherent worth and value as an individual and refusing to allow anyone or anything to hold you back from reaching your dreams. Doing this requires courage, resilience, and an unflinching willingness to challenge status quo beliefs, but the rewards can be immense in personal fulfillment.

INNER STRENGTH, CONFIDENCE, AND SELF-WORTH

Regaining our inner strength, confidence, and self-worth is essential for personal growth and development. When we believe in ourselves and our abilities, we're more likely to take risks, pursue passions, and realize goals. Conversely, lacking self-worth or confidence may hinder opportunities or lead us down paths less traveled, making life-altering decisions even harder than before.

Regaining inner strength, confidence, and self-worth can increase the ability to manage life's challenges, helping us face them with resilience. When facing setbacks or obstacles that threaten motivation or perseverance, confidence can keep us going through difficult situations without giving in to despair or giving in to discrimination or systemic barriers that stand in our way.

Note that rebuilding inner strength, confidence, and self-worth is not a one-time event. It requires ongoing efforts at self-reflection, caretaking, and deliberate action to develop these qualities and preserve them.

Regaining inner strength, confidence, and self-worth is essential to personal development, setting healthy boundaries, resilience, and facing life's challenges head-on. By tapping into these qualities we can overcome obstacles, pursue our passions more passionately, and lead fulfilling lives.

Today's world can be daunting and can often lead to an erosion of self-worth and confidence. Many factors contribute to these difficulties, including social and cultural pressures, unrealistic expectations, and gender stereotypes, all of which affect us differently but can equally damage both genders.

Men and women both face pressure to look a certain way in society, which can lead to body image issues and low self-esteem. Women, particularly, may feel the burden of unrealistic beauty standards that cause feelings of insecurity and self-doubt; men may experience similar pressure in terms of having certain physique characteristics or being dominant physically.

External pressures aside, both men and women face internal challenges as well. Self-doubt, impostor syndrome, and limiting beliefs can contribute to loss of self-confidence and worth, making these internal struggles hard to overcome without guidance and support from others. But with time comes hope. With practice we can learn to believe in ourselves and our abilities.

"Empower yourself. You are the only one who can."

Stacy London

CHAPTER *two*
SELF-DOUBT

Chapter 2

SELF-DOUBT

After my divorce, I struggled with feelings of doubt and inadequacy that made me question my worth and feel like something had been taken from me. I couldn't shake the feeling that somehow I had failed or wasn't good enough.

As I sat alone in reflection, I could not escape the depth of my self-doubt. It started in childhood as I witnessed my parents' turbulent marriage dissolve due to my father's alcoholism and verbal and emotional abuse my mother had to endured. Although I strived to build a better life, it seemed I couldn't break free of repeating their dysfunction; no matter how much I tried I just kept falling back into destructive habits and thought patterns.

My self-doubt manifested itself in various forms as I grew older. For twenty years I held on to an unsuccessful marriage that ultimately ended in failure, always striving to give my children the security I didn't have, regardless of what I had to endure. I had put my own needs aside to take care of my family. At times it felt like walking on eggshells, feeling unseen or afraid to speak up or ask for what I wanted.

Later, as I began living life without a partner, I realized how my self-doubt had damaged both my confidence and sense of worth. It became difficult for me to trust my judgment or my abilities, second-guessing myself at every turn and constantly making excuses for who I was made me question myself more and apologize more often for who I was becoming.

But I refused to allow self-doubt control me. Instead, I took steps to recognize its source and how it affected my life. At that time I didn't have the means to pay for therapy, I sought therapy through internet research and YouTube videos from therapists or coaches as well as support from friends and family. Furthermore, I made an effort to practice self-care and kindness toward myself when I made mistakes.

As time went by, I recognized how self-doubt was hindering my confidence and sense of worth. As soon as I understood this, I began taking risks, attempting new activities, and speaking up for myself.

Once I found my confidence and self-worth again, my life became richer and more fulfilling than I ever imagined. Self-doubt had been standing between myself and happiness and success. As soon as I knew this power laid within myself, I knew I could overcome any barrier it presented. As part of my journey of self-discovery I knew that anything I set my mind to was achievable!

I realized self-doubt is something most of us encounter at some point in our lives, from being uncertain of decisions to feeling inadequate with regard to skills or talents. Self-doubt can come in various forms ranging from uncertainty over decisions to feeling insufficient in one's abilities or talents.

One of the key aspects of self-doubt to keep in mind is its place within human experience. Everyone experiences some degree of it due to past failures, fear of the unknown, or negative feedback from others.

Self-doubt can have both positive and negative consequences. On one hand, self-doubt can help us become more deliberate and thoughtful with our decision-making and motivate us to work harder toward reaching our goals. To combat self-doubt effectively, we must identify its underlying causes and address them directly. Alternatively, it might help if one focused on their strengths instead of dwelling on perceived weaknesses or failures.

Overcoming self-doubt requires shifting from dwelling on limitations to considering one's potential and possibilities, with support and strategies from others, and ultimately reaching greater confidence and success in life.

WHAT CAUSES SELF-DOUBT IN OUR LIVES

Self-doubt can be a powerful force in our lives, often holding us back from reaching our true potential. Although self-doubt may be difficult to recognize and overcome, it is vitally important that we understand its origins and manifestation in our lives in order to find ways of managing it more effectively.

It often stems from external sources, including social expectations, criticism from others, or past experiences of failure. These external forces can become internalized as self-criticism, constant reminders of our flaws and limitations. This internalized voice of criticizing ourselves may become difficult to suppress, having an adverse effect on confidence and self-worth.

Self-doubt can prevent us from reaching our full potential. When we question ourselves, it may lead to reduced risks taken or attempts made due to fear of failure or rejection. Doubt also erodes confidence and self-esteem, which impacts relationships—for example, being reluctant to assert ourselves or express opinions can result in missed opportunities or feelings of regret. These beliefs become deeply embedded, leading us to think that success or happiness are unworthy pursuits, and our negative self-talk becomes reality.

To successfully overcome self-doubt, it's essential to recognize it is part of life. We all experience moments of doubt at some point or another, and it doesn't define us. By acknowledging doubts and fears we can begin challenging them and cultivate more optimistic and realistic views of ourselves.

We should focus on our strengths and accomplishments. By acknowledging even small accomplishments, we can build confidence and self-worth. Furthermore, it may help to practice self-compassion by treating ourselves with kindness rather than harsh self-critique.

Reaching out for help from a coach, loved ones, or support groups can also be immensely helpful when trying to combat self-doubt by connecting with others who understand our experiences and offer encouragement and strength to overcome our doubts and reaching our goals.

THE IMPACT OF SELF-DOUBT ON OUR SELF-WORTH AND CONFIDENCE

Self-doubt can have devastating repercussions for our confidence and self-worth, creating feelings of impostor syndrome and lack of self-belief that make life hard, making it difficult to pursue our passions and accomplish goals.

It can lead to a negative self-image in which we view ourselves as unworthy or undeserving of success and happiness, further amplifying feelings of doubt. This cycle creates self-defeating thoughts and behaviors.

Self-doubt can negatively impact our relationships with others. It may make it more difficult to trust others, leading to feelings of isolation and loneliness. Furthermore, self-doubt may hinder effective communication by prompting us to hold back from sharing thoughts or opinions for fear of being judged or rejected by others.

It can prevent us from taking risks and realizing our dreams, leaving us fearful of failure or uncertain in our abilities, thus stopping us from taking necessary steps toward meeting our goals.

Self-doubt's devastating impact on confidence and self-worth does not discriminate based on gender or age. Men and women, young and old, may be subject to it and its detrimental ramifications.

However, by acknowledging the impact of self-doubt in our lives and taking steps to overcome it, we can take steps toward recovery. I aim to offer practical techniques and insights to readers for building self-confidence and overcoming self-doubt. Through cultivating self-acceptance, self-love, and self-respect, we can free ourselves from negative self-talk and limiting beliefs while accepting ourselves fully for who we are. This allows for newfound purpose, confidence, and determination when pursuing goals and dreams with renewed strength and determination!

Self-doubt can be identified and overcome through different strategies. One technique involves identifying its source. Whether external sources or internal beliefs are causing doubt, beginning the process of questioning those beliefs and replacing them with positive affirmations can be helpful.

Reframing our negative self-talk can also help. Instead of criticizing ourselves, practicing self-compassion and speaking to ourselves as though you would a friend can shift focus away from perceived weaknesses and failures, and more toward strength and accomplishments.

Understanding the source of self-doubt and employing strategies to overcome it are keys to recovering our inner strength, confidence, and sense of worth. By silencing internal critics we can step more fully into our power as an individual ready to pursue passions and reach goals.

Practice mindfulness and self-awareness. Staying present in the moment enables us to observe our thoughts and emotions without judgment, as well as recognize when self-doubt may be entering. Being aware can help break up negative thought cycles with positive ones that bring out our best selves.

Another strategy is seeking support from others. By sharing our struggles with others, we can gain perspective and encouragement—and realize we are not alone in experiencing difficulties.

Set reasonable goals and take baby steps toward reaching them. Breaking larger goals down into manageable steps helps build momentum toward reaching success, and celebrating our small achievements helps boost self-confidence and reinforce positive beliefs about ourselves.

Remind yourself that self-doubt is part of life and should not be seen as an indicator that we are weak or inadequate. By acknowledging self-doubt as it exists and taking steps to address it, we can build greater resilience, self-confidence, and lead more fulfilling lives.

"Self-doubt kills more dreams than failure ever will."

Suzy Kassem

CHAPTER
three
LIMITING BELIEFS

Chapter 3
LIMITING BELIEFS

My entire life I had prioritized others over myself. From an early age I was taught to put others before myself and prioritize serving and taking care of others' needs before my own. Growing up hearing things like "Learn how to do laundry for when you get married," or "Learn to cook for your future husband," as if my worth solely hinged upon becoming a wife or mother. While these roles held great appeal for me personally, deep inside I knew there was more to me than simply these roles.

Retrospectively, what I needed to be taught was how to cook and do laundry for myself. These are essential skills we all require in order to become self-reliant. Not that this implies neglecting acts of service or caring for others; instead, this recognition highlights the significance of taking care of oneself first. This is something that I had neglected all along, unknowingly restricting my growth and potential.

I had always wanted to advance in my career or start my own business but had held back due to feeling inadequately qualified or worthy enough. I thought a college degree or enough money were essential prerequisites to achieve such ambitions. Neither were available.

However, I soon began to recognize how my own self-limiting beliefs were holding me back from reaching my true potential. So, I began questioning and challenging these beliefs until eventually discovering I possessed many talents and abilities that I hadn't previously appreciated.

In addition, I started practicing positive self-talk and affirmations daily. I would tell myself I was capable, strong, and worthy, visualizing myself excelling at work or my business and meeting my goals.

My mindset began to shift, and I began believing in myself and recognizing various aspects of myself. These included creative abilities (generating new ideas), critical thinking (analyzing information to evaluate arguments), commitment and reliability (always meeting obligations), being trustworthy as I fulfill responsibilities, and being an inspirational leader who guides others toward a common goal.

After facing over a year of uncertainty and fear, not knowing how I was going to do life on my own, this newfound belief gave me strength. Recognizing the value and significance of my career commitment over eighteen years in the healthcare sector, I summoned the courage to pursue higher roles, successfully landing a leading role that had doubled my income, reaching my goal of becoming a six-figure earner. I even managed to negotiate a signing bonus! At last I reached a level of income that provided financial security for myself and my children.

Without challenging my self-limiting beliefs, I never would have applied for the position that changed my life giving me a great peace of mind. Through positive self-talk and affirmations I gained the courage to leave my comfort zone, pursue new opportunities, and realize my full potential.

My story serves as a powerful reminder of the significance of confronting our limiting beliefs and practicing positive self-talk and affirmation techniques so as to overcome our doubts and fears and achieve our goals and dreams.

Limiting beliefs are negative thoughts or perceptions we hold about ourselves, others, or the world at large that prevent us from reaching our full potential. Common examples include *I'm not good enough*, *I can't do it*, or *I don't deserve success*. Removing these limiting beliefs from your life takes effort but can unlock its full potential with dedication and commitment. Replacing negative self-talk with positive, empowering ones will allow you to unlock more success and have more fulfilled life!

Unleashing myself from these self-limiting beliefs has been an incredible journey for me. Through it all I've realized that my worth doesn't lie solely within marriage or my ability to meet others' expectations. Instead I have talents, dreams, and aspirations all my own that define who I am as an individual. Through embracing my individuality and prioritizing self-care, I have experienced an unprecedented sense of empowerment and gained the courage to pursue my own passions. Although the process can be lengthy, my commitment is strong as I work toward breaking free from societal norms and accepting myself fully as an individual. By prioritizing my needs while simultaneously fulfilling others' needs, I am creating a more fulfilling and authentic life where I can flourish fully, leading me closer to reaching my full potential.

LIMITING BELIEFS PREVENT US FROM REACHING OUR TRUE POTENTIAL

Have you ever felt like something is keeping you from reaching your goals? Do you find yourself constantly second-guessing yourself or questioning decisions made in the past? If this sounds familiar, limiting beliefs could be at play.

Limiting beliefs are deeply-held attitudes and assumptions we hold about ourselves, others, and the world at large. These thoughts and assumptions can be conscious or unconscious based on past experiences, cultural conditioning, or opinions from outside sources. They act as barriers against taking risks, following passions, or reaching our full potential. Limiting beliefs often take the form of *I'm not smart enough*, *I don't have enough experience*, or even *I'm unworthy of success*.

Limiting beliefs have the ability to become self-fulfilling prophecies. When we believe we are incapable of accomplishing something, we may become less likely to pursue that goal and more likely to procrastinate, find excuses, or forgo challenges altogether, which can lead us down a path toward missed opportunities and hindered personal development.

Limiting beliefs can have a devastating effect on our self-esteem and confidence. If we constantly tell ourselves we aren't good enough, this becomes part of our identity, leading us toward feelings of inadequacy, anxiety, or depression.

To overcome limiting beliefs, be sure to recognize and challenge them. If you believe that starting your own business is beyond you, an effective way of challenging that belief could be speaking with other successful entrepreneurs who have navigated through similar hurdles successfully.

Attracting supportive people who can encourage and motivate you is also beneficial. Focusing on your strengths, accomplishments, and setting attainable goals can help build a more positive mindset and help overcome limiting beliefs that have limited your success in life. By freeing yourself of these beliefs you can unleash your full potential and achieve lasting success!

Break free of self-limiting beliefs and create an empowering mindset by employing these four techniques.

1. Recognize your negative self-talk: The first step toward uncovering limiting beliefs is becoming aware of your self-talk. Pay close attention when faced with challenges or opportunities, noting the thoughts that arise in response. Are they positive and supportive, or critical and self-defeating? During difficult situations or experiences, make a mental note to write down any negative ones and evaluate them objectively later.

2. Challenge your assumptions: After you've identified any negative thoughts, challenge them. Ask yourself if they are true or just assumptions you made from past experiences. Look for evidence that disproves any limiting beliefs you hold on to, and use this to reframe your mindset.

3. Shift your thoughts: Instead of dwelling on what you can't do, focus instead on what you can. Reframe limiting beliefs as affirming statements that reflect your strengths and potential. For instance, instead of saying, *I can't do this*, say instead *I am capable of learning and growing*.

4. Practice visualization: Visualization can be an incredibly effective tool for shifting your mindset. Dedicate five to ten minutes a day to visualizing yourself achieving your objectives and leading the life you envision, while visualizing yourself overcoming challenges along the way and triumphantly rising above them all.

Breaking free from self-limiting beliefs may not always be easy, but it is vital for living an abundant and meaningful life. By becoming aware of negative self-talk, challenging assumptions, reframing thoughts, and visualizing goals while seeking support, you can establish more empowering thought patterns. Through positive self-talk and affirmations practices you can program your subconscious with beliefs and attitudes that support your goals and lead to greater success in whatever endeavors you undertake.

RECOGNIZING OUR LIMITING BELIEFS AND RE-FRAMING THEM

Recognizing our limiting beliefs is the first step to breaking free from them. Here are four techniques that can help recognize limiting beliefs.

1. Self-reflection: Take some time to reflect on your thoughts and emotions, specifically regarding any beliefs holding you back or having an effect on your life. Are there any recurring negative thoughts or behavioral patterns you observe that need addressing?

2. Journaling: Writing down your thoughts and emotions can be an effective way to recognize limiting beliefs. Try being as honest and specific as possible when recording any fears, doubts, insecurities, or inadequacies you experience. Search for any patterns that emerge in the narrative.

3. Mindfulness: By practicing mindfulness, you can gain greater awareness of your thoughts and emotions in the present moment. If a negative thought or emotion arises, take a step back to observe it without judgment and determine its source. Perhaps an underlying belief may be at play?

4. Seek feedback from others: It can be hard to recognize our own limiting beliefs. So seek the opinion of friends, family, and colleagues regarding your strengths and weaknesses—they might help identify areas in which you might be hindering yourself.

Once you've identified your limiting beliefs, the next step should be recasting them in more positive terms. Here are four techniques that can help.

1. Positive affirmations: The practice of using positive affirmations is repeating positive statements to yourself daily to counteract any negative self-talk and reinforce positive beliefs about yourself—such as *I am capable of reaching my goals*, or *I deserve respect and love*.

2. Visualization: Visualization is a technique wherein one imagines themselves achieving their goals and living their ideal lifestyle, helping to build confidence and foster positive thoughts and beliefs. Try picturing yourself succeeding in your chosen field or living the ideal lifestyle as part of this practice.

3. Cognitive restructuring: Cognitive restructuring involves challenging negative thoughts and replacing them with more positive ones. Whenever a negative thought arises, ask yourself whether there is evidence supporting it, and then attempt to reframe the thought in an accurate yet more constructive manner.

4. Gratitude: Expressing gratitude can help you focus on the positive aspects of life and foster an optimistic attitude. Take time each day to jot down what makes you thankful, no matter how small.

By identifying and reframing limiting beliefs, you can unlock your full potential and meet your goals. Although it takes time and effort, eventually you will overcome mental barriers to living the life you envision for yourself.

POSITIVE SELF-TALK AND AFFIRMATIONS ARE POWERFUL PRACTICES

Positive self-talk is another effective strategy to build your mindset and reach your goals. It involves actively monitoring your thoughts and replacing negative self-talk with more encouraging statements. For instance, if you find yourself thinking *I can't do this*, replace that thought with: *I can do it, and I will succeed!*

Positive self-talk can help strengthen your confidence, decrease anxiety and stress levels, boost motivation and focus, create a more optimistic outlook on life, and enhance overall well-being. To incorporate positive self-talk into your daily routine, start by becoming aware of any negative self-talk that arises in your mind. Pay close attention to any demeaning statements or thoughts that cross your mind. Once these have been identified, replace them with positive statements consciously.

Positive self-talk and affirmations cannot be overemphasized. Positive affirmation statements provide you with a way of programming your subconscious mind with positive beliefs and attitudes. An example of an affirmation is: *I believe in my abilities and decisions and am thankful for all the blessings in my life.* Repeat affirmations daily either aloud or mentally. Soon they will become an integral part of your mindset and help you break free from self-limiting beliefs.

Positive self-talk and affirmations can help you shift away from negative thinking patterns by replacing them with positive ones, increasing self-confidence and motivation while improving overall well-being. With practice, your subconscious mind can be rewired to focus on positive outcomes and possibilities while letting go of limiting beliefs and self-doubt to unlock your full potential and build the life you truly desire.

Acclimatizing yourself to positive self-talk and affirmations may take time and practice, but the rewards far outweigh any effort involved. By training your mind to focus on positive thoughts and beliefs, you can increase self-esteem, build resilience, and achieve your goals more quickly and effortlessly.

"Your beliefs about what's possible will always limit what you can achieve."

Chris Witty

CHAPTER *four*
INNER STRENGTH

Chapter 4
INNER STRENGTH

Being someone who has experienced rock bottom, feeling lost and disoriented, I know how important it is to tap into our inner strength while simultaneously nurture self-awareness and self-compassion to navigate this challenging time in one's life.

After my heart was broken and my marriage ended, I felt confused and uncertain of my future. I had spent so many years with my partner that I didn't know who I was without them. I struggled with feelings of sadness, anger, and loneliness and I found it hard to move on. I wanted to focus on myself, and become whole on my own.

As I realized my inner strength would help me cope with these difficult circumstances, I worked on increasing self-awareness and compassion toward myself. To begin this process, I engaged in mindfulness and meditation practices that enhanced my awareness of thoughts and emotions as well as acceptance of myself despite any difficulty I was encountering.

As I turned my focus toward myself and my strengths and passions, I began exploring them more fully and finding fulfillment. New hobbies brought purpose and fulfillment as I discovered admirable qualities about myself, which caused me to appreciate myself more deeply.

As I increased self-awareness and self-compassion, I also learned how to let go of the past, both for myself and my former partner. I realized that holding on to anger or resentment would only cause more suffering, therefore I must let these feelings go in order to be truly happy.

Through this process I found the strength to rebuild my life after divorce. I started a new position at work, pursued real estate sales on the side, met new friends, and discovered one of the greatest and most fulfilling relationships imaginable: self-love. Without connecting to my inner strength and developing self-awareness and self-compassion I could have never accomplished such goals.

At times, going through a breakup can be painful and emotionally taxing yet also can offer opportunities for personal growth and self-discovery. While difficult at the time, breakups may actually present themselves as gifts if we use this time to connect with ourselves and build self-awareness and self-compassion. These traits will enable us to overcome challenges like these more efficiently, emerging stronger than before and more resilient as a result.

Recognizing and tapping into your inner strength can be a profoundly transformative process that can help you overcome challenges, reach goals, and live an overall more satisfying life. At its core, embracing one's inner strength means taking note of all of the unique qualities, talents, and abilities that define oneself, then harnessing those assets toward reaching one's fullest potential.

One of the key steps toward tapping into your inner strength is identifying your strengths and weaknesses. Take time to reflect upon past experiences, your successes and failures. What skills did you employ to overcome challenges and reach goals? In what areas do you struggle? By understanding both more fully, identifying them allows for a more personalized plan for personal development.

Release your inner strength by adopting a growth-oriented mindset. See challenges as opportunities rather than barriers or insurmountable obstacles. When faced with tough situations, ask yourself what can be learned, and use your strengths to overcome it. By cultivating such an optimistic outlook on life, you can develop resilience and the confidence necessary for taking on even the toughest of obstacles head-on.

Create a positive mindset by cultivating self-compassion. Treating yourself with kindness and empathy as you would treat a friend can go a long way toward cultivating resilience and building self-confidence and bolstering inner strength. When mistakes or setbacks occur, remind yourself that being imperfect is okay and that failure is part of learning process. Be kind and patient to yourself so you can discover inner strength!

Attaining inner strength requires taking action. This means setting goals, devising plans to meet them, and taking consistent, focused steps toward their fulfillment, whether personal or professional goals. By making progress toward your goals you'll build momentum and gain the confidence needed to keep moving forward.

Engaging your inner strength is a transformative experience that can help you navigate life's obstacles, meet goals, and live more fully. By understanding your strengths and weaknesses, adopting a positive attitude, cultivating self-compassion, and taking steps toward your goals, you can build resilience and gain the confidence to fulfill all of your potential.

CONNECTING WITH OUR INNER STRENGTH

Life is filled with challenges that can stretch us to our limit and push us beyond our abilities. In difficult moments, it may feel as if all is lost; however, each person has the inner strength that can help overcome adversity and reach our goals.

Reaching our inner strength requires self-awareness and self-compassion. To do this, it's necessary to recognize our own individual strengths and qualities and learn to value and accept ourselves for who we are. This can be accomplished using various techniques such as meditation, journaling, and positive self-talk.

Meditation can be a powerful way to deepen self-awareness and mindfulness. By quieting our minds and focusing on breathing, meditation can help us better tune in with our thoughts, emotions, and physical sensations. Through regular practice we can observe these inner experiences without judgment or attachment and gain a better understanding of who we truly are.

Journaling can be an excellent way to increase self-awareness and compassion, providing us with clarity about ourselves as we gain a greater understanding of our inner worlds. Journaling also serves as a useful means of self-reflection and expression, helping us process emotions in healthy, constructive ways.

Positive self-talk is an easy and effective way to foster compassion and confidence within ourselves. By choosing to acknowledge our strengths and accomplishments consciously, we can shift from focusing on self-doubt and negativity toward acceptance and positivity in our mindsets. Furthermore, positive self-talk can be used to counteract negative thoughts or beliefs as well as view challenges as opportunities for growth and learning.

By forging deeper connections to ourselves, we can tap into our inner strength and find courage and resilience to face life's obstacles head-on.

One way we can tap into our inner strength is through physical exercise. Exercise not only strengthens our bodies but also our minds, helping develop mental toughness and resilience as well as pushing through discomfort to overcome obstacles. Engaging in regular physical activity also has other positive side effects, like improving our mood and overall well-being, further reinforcing inner strength.

One key step toward tapping our inner strength is developing a positive mindset and attitude. This involves acknowledging all that is good in our lives, practicing gratitude, reframing negative experiences in a more constructive manner, and viewing negative events more positively. By adopting such an outlook we can foster greater resilience, inner strength, optimism, and hopefulness toward life itself.

Engaging our inner strength requires a dedication to personal growth and self-improvement, including developing self-awareness and compassion, as well as trusting in ourselves and our abilities. In doing so, we can overcome challenges, reach goals more easily, and live more fulfilling and meaningful lives.

Once we have developed a strong sense of self-awareness and compassion for ourselves, we can start drawing from our inner resources when facing challenges. Here are four effective strategies.

1. Remind yourself of your strengths: When faced with difficult situations, reminding yourself of your individual strengths can help build up confidence and motivate you. Additionally, this gives the courage needed to take the necessary actions.

2. Build self-care into your routine: Nurturing yourself is essential to building inner strength. Make sure that your physical and emotional well-being takes priority by ensuring you get enough sleep, eating a nutritious diet, engaging in regular physical exercise sessions, and participating in activities that bring joy.

3. Establish boundaries: Boundaries are essential to protecting our inner strength and emotional balance. By setting boundaries, it becomes easier to say no to things that drain energy or compromise values while prioritizing activities and relationships that align with your goals and values.

4. Seek support: When seeking assistance is necessary, do not hesitate. Whether it means talking with trusted confidantes and family members, seeking professional counseling advice, or joining support groups, there are various resources available that can assist in managing tough circumstances.

Releasing our inner strength is necessary to successfully managing life's challenges and reaching our goals. Through building self-awareness, compassion, and tapping into our individual strengths and qualities we can develop the resilience necessary to confront obstacles head-on and create the life we wish for ourselves.

BUILDING SELF-AWARENESS AND SELF-COMPASSION

Self-awareness and self-compassion are indispensable components of personal development and well-being. By increasing self-awareness and cultivating self-compassion, they enable us to gain a better understanding of ourselves, our emotions, behaviors, and how they impact each other, as well as boosting self-acceptance and love for oneself. Below are five techniques for building these essential attributes of wellness.

1. Mindfulness meditation: Mindfulness meditation can be an excellent way to enhance self-awareness and self-compassion. By focusing on the present moment without judgment or distraction, mindfulness practice helps increase your awareness of thoughts, emotions, and bodily sensations, thus developing greater acceptance and compassion toward yourself and others.

2. Journaling: Writing in a journal can help you process your emotions and gain a deeper insight into yourself. Use it to reflect upon past experiences, identify patterns in behavior, and explore feelings and beliefs. Regular journaling sessions also promote greater self-compassion by accepting flaws as part of who you are.

3. Therapy: Therapy can be an invaluable way of developing greater self-awareness and compassion for oneself. A trained therapist can assist in exploring your thoughts and emotions, identifying patterns in behavior, and developing new coping strategies.

Therapy may also validate experiences while offering a safe space for self-reflection.

4. Reflecting: Reflecting on past experiences and behaviors can help foster greater self-awareness and compassion for yourself. Regular self-reflection can also foster increased acceptance and appreciation of any flaws or imperfections you might discover within yourself.

5. Positive self-talk: Positive self-talk involves replacing negative and unfavorable self-talk with positive, affirming statements in order to promote an attitude of kindness toward yourself while increasing both your self-esteem and confidence levels.

By including these techniques into your daily routine, you can develop greater self-awareness and compassion while improving overall well-being and quality of life.

TAPPING INTO OUR INNER STRENGTH

Here are four effective strategies for tapping into your inner strength when facing challenges.

1. Reframe negative thoughts: When faced with challenges it can be easy to slip into negative thought patterns. To harness your inner strength and foster growth, try reframing negative statements such as *I can't do this* into more empowering ones such as *I know there is a way*.

2. Create a support system: Establishing a network of friends, family, and/or a coach can help you tap into your inner strength when facing challenges. They can offer encouragement, guidance, and emotional support when necessary.

3. Cultivate gratitude: By cultivating gratitude, it can help shift your focus from what is missing to all of the positive resources available to you. Practicing it regularly can strengthen inner resilience by reminding you of all that life offers you.

4. Set achievable goals: Setting achievable goals can be an excellent way to harness your inner strength by giving you a sense of direction and purpose. When facing challenges, set small, attainable goals daily that you can work toward. This will give a sense of progress and accomplishment that can help build confidence and resilience.

By adopting these strategies into your lifestyle, you can tap into your inner strength and develop resilience and courage necessary for facing life's obstacles with grace.

Rise Above and Own Your Power

"True strength is the courage to keep pushing forward, even when the odds seem overwhelming."

Unknown

CHAPTER *five*
CONFIDENCE

Chapter 5
CONFIDENCE

To regain and develop my confidence, I looked at my interests and decided to get involved in real estate sales. I started networking, hosting open houses and meeting new clients, something I had always wanted to do but had been too afraid to try. As I interacted with new people I improved my social skills, I began to feel more confident in other areas of my life as well.

I had become dependent of the idea of my spouse's emotional support and validation. Without it, I felt lost and uncertain of myself, fearful to take risks or pursue goals because I didn't trust myself to pursue them.

But as time passed, I began to recognize that confidence comes from within; it cannot be given by others. So I made an effort to build my self-esteem and worthiness by pushing myself past my comfort zone and exploring new experiences.

As I made an active effort to surround myself with positive, supportive people who believed in me, my relationships strengthened significantly with family and friends who could relate to my experience and provided much-needed guidance and advice as I navigated my new life.

As I worked to gain confidence, I began experiencing positive personal and professional changes. No longer was I afraid to speak up in meetings or take on new responsibilities at work. Dating seemed exciting, full of new adventures, interesting people, and meaningful connections!

Looking back over my journey, I recognize the value of confidence for personal and professional success. While confidence doesn't come easily to everyone, it can be fostered through daily practices like building it through positive influences. By prioritizing building my confidence and surrounding myself with supportive people, I emerged stronger and more resilient than ever.

Confidence is essential to both personal and professional success. It refers to trust in yourself, believing in your abilities and qualities, as well as being confident about being able to overcome challenges and reach goals.

Confidence isn't something you're born with; it is an ability that can be developed with deliberate effort and practice. In this chapter we will examine the role confidence plays in personal and professional success, techniques for building and maintaining it, and body language as a form of nonverbal communication as well as its effect on success.

PERSONAL AND PROFESSIONAL SUCCESS

Confidence is essential to personal and professional success. It allows you to take on new challenges, learn from past errors, and mature as an individual. Being confident increases the likelihood that you will take initiative, be assertive when making decisions, and align them with your goals and values. Furthermore, it allows you to become more resilient in the face of setbacks, helping you recover faster after setbacks occur.

Confidence plays a critical role in both personal and professional success by shaping how we perceive ourselves and how others see us. Confident people tend to feel more competent, capable, and in control of their lives. Those with confidence tend to pursue their dreams more aggressively and are more likely to take calculated risks.

Confidence in the workplace is vitally important, as it can dramatically impact your career trajectory. Confident employees tend to be promoted faster, earn higher salaries, and be given additional responsibilities within their organizations as they can take charge of projects themselves and work autonomously while making informed decisions that ultimately benefit all parties involved.

Conversely, those lacking confidence often struggle to reach their goals or advance in their careers. They may fear speaking up, taking on new challenges, or asserting themselves in the workplace, which can result in missed opportunities, decreased job satisfaction, and an overall sense of emptiness on personal and professional levels.

Confidence is something that can be developed and strengthened. Some strategies to build it include setting realistic goals, learning new skills, practicing self-care, and seeking support from friends or coach if you find yourself doubting yourself and low on self-esteem.

Confidence is an essential component of personal and professional success. It impacts how you perceive yourself, how others view you, and your ability to reach your goals. By building and maintaining confidence, you can enhance performance, create more opportunities, and lead a more fulfilling life.

Confidence isn't something you can build overnight; it takes effort and practice to develop and keep. Here are seven proven techniques for building and sustaining it.

1. Establish realistic objectives: Setting achievable goals and celebrating each achievement can build confidence gradually, giving you the chance to experience success while building momentum, which ultimately increases motivation.

2. Add self-compassion into your routine: Self-compassion refers to being kind and understanding toward oneself during times of struggle or defeat, acknowledging imperfections as well as providing support and encouragement in order to build resilience and confidence.

3. Accept failure: Mistakes are part of life's learning journey and should be seen as opportunities to improve yourself and gain greater self-confidence. Reframing failure as an opportunity for development will help foster a growth mindset while building your self-assurance.

4. Visualize success: Visualization can be an incredibly powerful way of building confidence and motivation. Simply visualizing yourself successfully completing a task or reaching a goal creates a mental blueprint and strengthens confidence that it's achievable.

5. Acquire new skills: Expanding your knowledge and abilities can boost your self-confidence. Attend classes, read books, or participate in workshops to acquire new skills can expand your abilities while increasing confidence levels.

6. Engage in positive self-talk: Your dialogue can have a tremendous impact on your confidence level. Rather than criticizing yourself, try practicing positive self-talk by emphasizing your strengths and achievements. This can help create a more positive outlook and boost self-assurance.

7. Surround yourself with supportive people: Who you spend your time with can make a profound difference on your confidence level. Seek supportive friends, family members, or colleagues who can provide encouragement, validation, and constructive criticism as needed.

Building confidence requires cultivating self-compassion. Self-compassion means treating yourself with kindness, understanding, and acceptance while acknowledging any mistakes or shortcomings without judgment. Be gentle with your own feelings and feedback as you strive for improvement. By practicing self-compassion you can cultivate a more positive self-image that in turn boosts confidence.

Building and sustaining confidence takes intentionality and practice. Setting achievable goals, practicing self-compassion, accepting failure gracefully, learning new skills, practicing positive self-talk, surrounding yourself with supportive people, and taking care of yourself are all ways that you can establish and nurture confidence.

BODY LANGUAGE AND NONVERBAL COMMUNICATION

Body language and nonverbal communication can have an immense influence on our confidence levels. Your posture, facial expressions, and tone of voice all play essential roles in conveying to others how much confidence you feel as well as how you feel internally. Here are five tips for using these forms of nonverbal communication to build your internal sense of pride.

1. Stand up straight: Your posture speaks volumes about the level of confidence that lies within. Putting forth good posture demonstrates this to others—and can have a profound effect on how you feel about yourself. To project confidence and assurance, stand tall, with shoulders back and chin up. Your shoulders should move back slightly when standing up straight.

2. Make eye contact: Eye contact is an indicator of confidence and engagement, so look at people in the eye when speaking with them and maintain eye contact throughout your conversation. It can help establish rapport and build trust among individuals.

3. Adopt an assured tone of voice: Speaking clearly and confidently can convey your level of self-assurance to others while increasing your internal sense of confidence. Employ a firm, assertive tone when speaking.

4. Smile: Smiling can help you feel more at ease and approachable while simultaneously exuding confidence and positivity to others. A smile conveys warmth, friendliness, and confidence and creates an inviting and pleasant environment for conversation and connection between individuals.

5. Avoid nervous habits: Nervous habits like fidgeting, tapping, or avoiding eye contact may signal anxiety or low self-confidence. Be conscious of these habits and work toward eliminating them.

Confident body language includes standing up straight, making eye contact, and using assertive gestures to display your confidence and capability to others and build your own confidence levels in return. Positive body language techniques will show others you are assertive and capable, something that may increase theirs as well.

By utilizing confident body language and nonverbal communication techniques, you can not only convey confidence to others but also boost your own internal sense of security. These behaviors may become part of your routine to help make you feel more capable in all areas of your life.

BUILDING CONFIDENCE

Confidence is essential to personal and professional success. It helps individuals face challenges head-on, seize opportunities when presented, and pursue their goals successfully. Without confidence, life would be much harder. Cultivating it requires deliberate and consistent effort toward developing a positive outlook and an increased sense of self-worth. Cultivating confidence involves developing a positive sense of self-worth, trusting in your abilities, and having the courage to take risks and pursue your goals. Here are six effective strategies for increasing confidence.

1. Recognize and advance your strengths: By taking an introspective view and acknowledging your strengths and talents, you're more likely to feel capable and secure about who you are as an individual. Building upon and exploiting them, as well as focusing on improving them, may even increase feelings of confidence and capability in you.

2. Fight negative self-talk: Negative self-talk can erode confidence and self-esteem, so when you detect you are having negative thoughts or beliefs about yourself, combat them with positive affirmations or evidence against them.

3. Set achievable goals: Establishing achievable goals can help boost confidence by giving an immediate sense of achievement and progress.

4. Take action: By taking even small steps toward your goals, you can build your confidence by showing that you can reach them.

5. Prioritize self-care: Caring for your physical and emotional well-being can boost confidence. Make time for activities that make you feel good, such as exercise, meditation, or simply spending time with loved ones. When these important and basic elements combine, your confidence may naturally rise!

6. Accept failure and adopt a growth-oriented perspective on failure: Recognizing failure as an opportunity rather than as an indicator of your self-worth can help build resilience and boost confidence levels.

Create confidence by setting achievable goals. Setting goals provides direction and purpose, and reaching them gives a sense of accomplishment that boosts confidence. Setting realistic goals that are broken down into more manageable steps helps prevent feeling overwhelmed as you make steady progress toward your objectives.

Resilience is key to building confidence. Failure is an inevitable part of life—how we respond to it makes all the difference. By viewing failure as an opportunity for learning and growth, setbacks can become valuable lessons that help improve and drive overall performance. By accepting failure and being resilient enough to embrace it as part of a positive growth experience, confidence builds.

Cultivating confidence is integral to reaching both personal and professional success. By setting realistic goals, practicing self-compassion, accepting failure gracefully, visualizing success vividly, using confident body language and nonverbal communication techniques, and visualizing success, confidence can be built slowly. This–helps us overcome challenges, reach goals faster, and create lives we are proud to live!

"Confidence is not 'they will like me.' Confidence is 'I'll be fine if they don't."

Christina Grimmie

CHAPTER six
NAVIGATING OBSTACLES

Chapter 6
NAVIGATING OBSTACLES

When my life was turned upside-down, I found satisfaction and motivation by setting small goals and celebrating each of my achievements, no matter how small. Additionally, I made an effort to stay positive by surrounding myself with people who believed in me and supported my goals.

As I began this new chapter of my life, I faced many obstacles. Financial insecurity and the fear of becoming a single parent. Furthermore, having to depend on a single income to cover basic expenses such as housing, food, and healthcare was sometimes challenging to do alone.

But I was determined to overcome these hurdles and create a fulfilling and stable life for myself and my children. Recognizing that success required being resilient and adaptable, I began work on developing these qualities.

I found my best strategy was staying focused on my goals. For example, I wanted my daughter to graduate high school with her childhood friends rather than move during her final year of high school due to my divorce proceedings. Divorce involves many changes that can make a stable home seem unstable. I wanted as few changes to occur during this uncertain process to protect my children as much as possible and provide a stable home environment for them. I knew what it took for this to come true— nothing would deter me.

I managed to gather the courage to pursue a higher position in my career and pursued real estate sales in addition to my full-time job. At the same time, I made sure that self-care and enjoyment were always top of mind by exploring new activities, connecting with nature, pursuing my goals, and spending quality time with family and friends.

At times it wasn't easy, and there were moments where I wanted to give up, but by staying motivated and focused on my goals, I eventually managed to overcome any challenge.

My journey taught me that success lies not in avoiding obstacles but in learning how to overcome them. By remaining resilient and adaptable in pursuit of my goals, I was able to create an enjoyable life for me and my children.

If you're facing obstacles in your own life, remember that you can overcome them with resilience, adaptability, and an eye toward goals. Take control of your power! With that mindset you can accomplish anything your mind desires!

As we move through life and work, we often come up against numerous obstacles that threaten to derail our progress. These could range from social biases and stereotypes to personal setbacks or challenges. With resilience, adaptability, and the right strategies in place we can overcome them and remain focused on reaching our goals.

One key strategy for successfully navigating obstacles is developing a growth mindset. This involves seeing challenges as opportunities to gain experience and grow, rather than as barriers that must be surmounted. People with a growth mindset tend to persevere more readily when facing difficult circumstances because they understand that their abilities develop through hard work.

At times, success doesn't follow an expected path, and we may need to adjust our goals or approach when unexpected obstacles arise. Being open-minded to new ideas and approaches can help us find creative solutions to problems while staying on the path toward our goals.

Foster a supportive network of family, friends, and colleagues to provide encouragement and advice when facing obstacles. Finding mentors or role models who have navigated similar challenges successfully may prove particularly helpful, providing invaluable advice and assistance.

At all levels of health, we must care for ourselves physically and mentally. Living a healthy lifestyle, including regular exercise, healthy nutrition, and adequate rest, can help build resilience and mental fortitude to overcome obstacles in our life. Seeking professional counseling support may also be necessary to maintain mental well-being and maintaining overall wellness.

Navigating obstacles takes resilience, adaptability, and a growth mindset. By remaining flexible, seeking support, and taking care of ourselves when facing difficulties, we can overcome challenges more easily and stay on course toward reaching our goals.

RESILIENCE AND ADAPTABILITY

As we face life's obstacles and pursue our goals, resilience and adaptability must also be developed in ourselves. Resilience refers to the capacity to recover from difficulties or setbacks and persevere even when faced with adversity. Adaptability refers to finding creative ways of responding to changing conditions by adapting quickly. These skills are crucial in today's rapidly shifting and unpredictable environment.

To build resilience and adaptability, there are various steps we can take. First is cultivating a growth mindset—the belief that our skills and intellect can be improved with effort and perseverance. Also, engage in self-care by tending to our physical, emotional, and mental well-being. We should continue to seek new experiences or challenges and be open to feedback or constructive criticism. Mentors can be sources of guidance, encouragement, or inspiration.

Resilience and adaptability are particularly essential skills for women who frequently face unique obstacles in their personal and professional lives. Women may face discrimination, bias, obstacles to advancement in the workplace as well as pressure from society to conform to traditional gender roles. They also may find balancing career aspirations with family responsibilities challenging.

Resilience and adaptability are two essential characteristics that will enable us to overcome challenges and reach our goals. Resilience allows us to rebound quickly after setbacks or failures, learn from past errors, and persevere despite obstacles. Adaptability enables us to navigate changing circumstances to find opportunities for growth and success.

Resilience and adaptability can have far-reaching benefits beyond an individual success. Find others who can serve as role models and mentors for those who may be struggling to inspire and empower them to overcome challenges of their own. Furthermore, resilient and adaptable bring diverse perspectives to the table, contributing to innovation and creativity professionally and personally.

Resilience and adaptability are vital skills for those striving to thrive in today's rapidly shifting and unpredictable environment. By cultivating these abilities, we can overcome obstacles to our goals while acting as role models and contributing to greater societal progress.

STAYING MOTIVATED AND FOCUSED ON GOALS

Staying motivated and focused on our goals requires various strategies. Establish clear, specific, and attainable goals, and break them down into smaller steps. This can help keep us feel accomplished even during setbacks or challenges. This approach may keep us feeling positive while keeping motivation levels up.

Create an empowering sense of purpose and meaning in life. Being clear on our values and vision helps keep us focused and motivated even in the face of obstacles or distractions, while visualization and positive self-talk techniques can build resilience so that our goals don't slip from sight when facing difficulties or challenges.

Stay motivated and focused by celebrating successes and learning from failures. Recognizing our achievements can build confidence and momentum, keeping us going even when confronted with setbacks or challenges. By approaching failure with an attitude of continuous improvement, we can remain on track with our goals, overcoming any obstacles along the way.

Associating ourselves with supportive networks such as family, friends, and colleagues can provide encouragement, accountability, and an outlet for ideas or challenges we are facing. Mentors or role models who have reached similar goals may also prove beneficial; we can learn from their experience and strategies.

Cultivating a growth mindset can also be helpful, which involves accepting challenges as opportunities for personal growth and learning. By viewing setbacks as learning experiences rather than obstacles to progress toward our goals, we can stay motivated and continue moving in the right direction toward meeting them.

Staying motivated and focused means prioritizing self-care. This may involve engaging in activities that bring joy. By caring for both physical and mental health, taking better care can improve energy levels, decrease stress levels, and enhance overall well-being, ultimately increasing motivation and focus.

Staying organized and managing our time efficiently can bring many advantages. This may involve setting priorities, creating schedules and to-do lists, breaking larger tasks into manageable steps, or breaking them down further into manageable ones. By managing time effectively we can avoid feeling overwhelmed while remaining focused on our goals and priorities.

Staying motivated and on track with goals requires employing several strategies, such as setting clear goals, developing a sense of purpose, cultivating a growth mindset, prioritizing self-care, building a supportive network, and managing time effectively. When we employ these tactics effectively we can use them to overcome obstacles while still maintaining an ideal work-life balance and overall well-being.

"Success is not about avoiding obstacles, but about navigating through them with courage and determination."

Unknown

CHAPTER *seven* USING YOUR VOICE

Chapter 7
USING YOUR VOICE

If you find yourself feeling lost and uncertain after experiencing a significant life change such as a breakup or any major change, remember that you hold the power to create the life you desire. Rise above any feelings of helplessness and own your power. With practice and perseverance, you can find your voice, speak assertively, navigate difficult conversations and conflicts confidently, and find peace within yourself.

After spending over twenty years putting aside my needs and desires in order to make my marriage work, I had lost touch with who I was as an individual and my wants.

As I began rebuilding my life, it soon became clear to me that in order to create the life I desired I must learn how to advocate for myself and advocate for my needs.

At first, it was challenging. I had spent so many years of silencing my own voice and bowing to my ex-husband's wishes that I didn't know where to start. But I began to read books and attend workshops and I eventually learn to find my voice and gained confidence in assertively communicating.

I employed these techniques daily in my personal and professional lives. To begin, I started small by speaking up in meetings and asking for what I needed in my relationships.

I learned to listen actively and remain calm even during times of high emotion, focusing on finding solutions rather than assigning blame. Most importantly,

I learned how to stand up for myself and advocate for my needs—skills that I am still honing each day.

Through this process, I regained my self-esteem and sense of worthiness. I realized I could create the life I desired by advocating for myself.

Now I am enjoying a healthy and fulfilling relationship with myself, pursuing my goals and dreams with confidence and dedication. Self-love is truly the key to happiness. Once found, it will attract even more positivity in your life! Self-love increases confidence, resilience, and ability to manage life's challenges while simultaneously drawing in people who share your positivity outlook on life.

One of the most essential skills we can acquire is the ability to find and use our voice effectively. Voice can serve as an incredible platform for self-expression, advocacy, leadership, and personal and professional success, yet many struggle with finding theirs due to social conditioning, judgment or conflict fears, or lacking confidence in themselves or their abilities. This chapter explores this topic further while offering strategies and techniques for using it assertively in difficult conversations and conflicts.

Finding and using your voice means having the confidence and ability to express your opinions, needs, and ideas in an assertive and clear manner. It means being able to effectively communicate with others, whether personal or professional relationships, while assertively advocating for yourself and your ideas. Those who can find and use their voices more successfully tend to build successful careers, form meaningful relationships, and have an uplifting influence in their communities and the world at large.

To find and use your voice effectively, the first step should be identifying your values, beliefs, and goals.

This may involve reflecting upon past personal and professional experiences as well as areas in which you feel enthusiastic and motivated to make a change. Once you understand who you are as an individual, practicing more assertive expressing can begin in various situations.

One key strategy for effectively using your voice is communicating in an open and confident manner. This may mean using strong and direct language, speaking with conviction, and maintaining eye contact and good posture while speaking clearly and confidently. You could also try listening actively to others before responding in thoughtful fashion rather than defensively or impulsively.

An effective strategy for discovering and using your voice is self-advocacy, or representing oneself in matters pertaining to needs and interests and setting boundaries when necessary. Self-advocacy also involves looking out for growth opportunities as well as seeking support or feedback from others as needed.

Recognizing and challenging societal factors that prevent us from speaking out is also crucial, including gender bias, stereotypes, and cultural expectations. By understanding and challenging such obstacles to expression and making voices heard, we will feel empowered to express ourselves freely and make our voices be heard.

Finding and using one's voice are critical skills for seeking personal and professional success. By understanding our own values and goals, communicating assertively yet confidently, practicing self-advocacy, and breaking through social barriers, we can feel more empowered to have an impactful impact in the world.

SPEAKING UP AND ADVOCATING FOR OURSELVES

Here are five ways in which speaking out and advocating for ourselves can be powerful.

1. Foster self-confidence: By advocating for ourselves and recognizing our needs, we can demonstrate our appreciation of ourselves and our worth. This advocacy can build self-confidence and have a significant positive effect in all areas of our lives.

2. Set boundaries: By speaking up and standing up for ourselves, we can set clear boundaries that reflect our needs and expectations, helping avoid being taken advantage of or mistreated, and ensuring our relationships are based on mutual respect.

3. Advance our goals: When we advocate for ourselves, we can clearly articulate our goals and interests while taking steps that support them. This can help advance our careers, meet personal aspirations and goals, and create the lives we dream of.

4. Foster social change: When we advocate for ourselves and others who may be marginalized or underrepresented, this helps promote social change for a more equitable and just society.

5. Model positive behavior: By advocating for ourselves, we are setting an example that others may follow and creating an environment of assertiveness and self-advocacy in which others can find strength to do the same. This could potentially create an environment of assertiveness and self-advocacy among colleagues and friends alike.

Speaking up for ourselves is an integral component of self-expression and creating positive social change. Through finding and using our voice, we can foster an environment in which all voices are respected and appreciated.

FINDING OUR VOICE AND SPEAKING ASSERTIVELY

To find and use our voice effectively, it's essential that we identify our values, beliefs, and goals, then build the confidence and skills required to express them assertively. Here are eight techniques that can assist with this.

1. Engage in active listening: By actively listening and empathizing with others, we can gain a better understanding of their perspectives and needs, while building stronger relationships founded upon trust and respect.

2. Build self-awareness: Through self-reflection, we can increase self-awareness of our thoughts, emotions, and behaviors, identify our strengths and weaknesses, and develop more authentic and confident voices.

3. Employ "I" statements: By using "I" statements (e.g., "I feel frustrated when..."), we can express our thoughts and feelings without resorting to blame or attacking other parties.

4. Establish clear boundaries: By setting clear and assertive boundaries, we can protect our own interests and needs while avoiding being taken advantage of or mistreated by others.

5. Engage in mindful meditation: Through practicing mindful meditation and being present in the moment, we can decrease anxiety and self-doubt while developing the clarity and focus necessary to express ourselves with confidence and assertively.

6. Seeking feedback: Seeking feedback from trusted friends, family members, or mentors can give us invaluable insight into our communication style as well as pinpoint areas for improvement.

7. Role-play: Practicing assertive communication skills in an open and encouraging environment, such as with friends or at therapy, can help us build confidence while honing our communication abilities.

8. Leverage positive affirmations: By employing positive affirmations such as "I am confident in expressing my needs and values," we can reframe negative self-talk and build self-confidence.

By employing these techniques, we can gain the skills and confidence required to find our voices and express them authentically while building stronger relationships based on trust and respect.

DIFFICULT CONVERSATIONS AND CONFLICTS

Even when we have developed strong and assertive voices, we may still encounter challenging conversations and conflicts in our personal and professional lives. When these situations arise, approach each dialogue with empathy, respect, and an eye toward finding mutually agreeable solutions. Following are seven strategies that can assist with managing these discussions or conflicts.

1. Active listening: By actively and empathically listening to another's viewpoint, we can build trust and avoid miscommunication.

2. Reframe the conversation: By reframing our dialogue in a more positive or constructive manner, we can shift its focus from criticism and blame-shifting toward problem-solving and collaboration.

3. Assertive communication: By employing assertive communication techniques such as "I" statements and clear boundaries, we can express our needs and interests without attacking or blaming another party.

4. Discover common ground: By identifying areas of agreement or shared values, we can establish a foundation for productive dialogue and work toward finding mutually acceptable solutions.

5. Manage emotions: Emotions may run high during difficult conversations and conflicts, so we need to learn how to regulate our own and others' emotional responses proactively and systematically. Additionally, acknowledging and validating each person's emotional state should be prioritized as part of any solution plan.

6. Take a break: If a conversation becomes heated or unproductive, taking a short break and coming back later may help bring about greater understanding and productivity.

7. Recognize when to walk away: In certain situations, it may not be possible to find an amicable solution or communicate effectively with another party. When this occurs, it may be important to recognize when to disengage from a conversation or relationship altogether.

With these strategies in hand, we can approach difficult conversations and conflicts with confidence, empathy, and an eye on finding positive solutions that foster long-term peace.

Discovering and exercising our voices are crucial skills for personal and professional success, as well as building a more equitable society. By developing self-awareness, active listening skills, assertive communication techniques, and the ability to navigate difficult conversations more effectively we can become better communicators and advocates for ourselves and others alike.

Through words and actions we can challenge harmful beliefs or systems while increasing understanding and empathy and working toward positive change. Finding and using our voices is not just individual achievement but contributes toward making a better world together.

"Your voice is your unique gift to the world. Use it fearlessly and with purpose."

Oprah Winfrey

CHAPTER *eight*
STRONG RELATIONSHIPS

Chapter 8
STRONG RELATIONSHIPS

As I began rebuilding my life, I realized the significance of strong relationships in my success and happiness in the workplace and in my personal life. So I focused on strengthening and maintaining good ones with friends, family, and colleagues to increase fulfillment in my work and personal life. This had a direct positive effect on life itself!

An effective technique I found helpful for building relationships was being proactive and intentional in my interactions. I took time each day to reach out and offer support or assistance whenever needed, as well as express appreciation and thanks for others' contributions.

But I also realized the importance of setting boundaries and communicating effectively as I maintained strong relationships. Because I overcommitted myself and took on too much, at times I was feeling stressed and exhausted. It became important for me to set clear boundaries and communicate my needs and limitations to those around me.

I also realized the significance of active listening and empathic communication. By truly listening to others and showing an interest in their perspectives, I was able to build trusting relationships and strengthen them further.

By employing these genuine techniques and strategies, I was able to form an extremely supportive network of family, friends, and colleagues, which provides emotional support, professional advice, as well as opportunities for growth and development.

Looking back, I realized that each one of us holds the power to build and nurture healthy relationships. By being intentional about setting boundaries and communicating effectively, we can foster mutually beneficial relationships in both our personal and professional lives.

If you're having difficulty building or maintaining relationships in your own life, remember that everything starts with you. By being intentional about how you build and communicate these relationships, you too can build a solid support system that can help you thrive across every aspect of life.

Relationships are an essential element of our personal and professional lives, providing emotional support, helping to achieve our goals, and contributing to overall well-being. Whether we are building them with friends, family, colleagues, or clients, it's important to invest time and effort into developing strong ties, be they with friends, family, colleagues, or clients. In this chapter we will examine the role relationships play in our lives, techniques for creating strong bonds, as well as setting boundaries effectively and communicating effectively.

Building lasting relationships requires time, energy, and dedication. Doing so means respecting each individual's needs, values, perspectives, as well as being open and honest in our communication. Here are seven techniques for forging and maintaining strong relationships.

1. Active listening: Active listening involves paying close attention to what another person is telling you, comprehending their message, and responding appropriately. It means avoiding distractions such as phone calls and social media, asking pertinent questions, and summarizing what has been heard to ensure a complete understanding of their perspective.

2. Demonstrate empathy: Showing empathy means placing yourself in another person's shoes and understanding their feelings and emotions. Validate their emotions even if their viewpoint differs from yours.

3. Be honest and transparent: Honesty and transparency are the cornerstone of trust-building in relationships. Being truthful with yourself about your thoughts, feelings, and intentions, as well as acknowledging any mistakes, can only strengthen relationships.

4. Communicate effectively: Effective communication involves clearly and respectfully articulating your thoughts and emotions while actively listening to those you interact with. Avoid making assumptions, judgments, and criticism. Focus on finding common ground and solutions.

5. Develop rapport: Establishing rapport involves discovering shared interests and experiences, using them as the cornerstone for building the relationship. Being genuine, friendly, approachable, and showing sincere curiosity for their lives are all hallmarks of positive rapport-building practices.

6. Respect boundaries: Respecting boundaries means understanding and acknowledging another person's limits, preferences, and personal space. This involves seeking permission before sharing personal information, refraining from asking intrusive questions, and acknowledging when someone needs space or time alone.

7. Be reliable and dependable: Being consistent means being reliable, trustworthy, and dependable with your actions and words. Being on time for meetings, fulfilling commitments, and keeping promises are all hallmarks of reliability and dependability. This demonstrates that you respect the relationship and time of others.

Building strong relationships requires time, patience, and commitment. Through listening actively, showing empathy, being honest and transparent in communications, forming rapport with others effectively, respecting boundaries while being consistent we can build and strengthen bonds with those in our lives.

RELATIONSHIPS IN OUR PERSONAL AND PROFESSIONAL LIVES

Relationships play an essential role in our personal and professional lives. At home, relationships provide emotional support, companionship, and a sense of belonging that helps us navigate life's trials while celebrating its joys. At work, strong relationships help build an expansive network of contacts that advance careers while opening up doors to new opportunities with colleagues, clients, and supervisors. This leads to increased job satisfaction and fulfilling careers for everyone involved.

Strong relationships provide much more than emotional or professional support. Studies have demonstrated that people in strong relationships tend to enjoy better physical and mental health outcomes. They tend to experience less depression, anxiety, and other forms of mental challenges while living longer and healthier lives due to these important bonds providing us with purpose, meaning, and feeling supported and cared for.

Relationships play an integral part in our personal lives, whether friendships, romantic partnerships, or familial bonds. Some relationships provide love, intimacy, and belonging. Others present opportunities for personal growth and self-discovery. For instance, being in a romantic partnership can teach us compromise, communication, and commitment. Being a parent teaches patience, responsibility, and unconditional love.

Professional relationships are vitally important in creating a solid network and furthering our careers. Strong bonds between colleagues, clients, and supervisors can open doors to new opportunities that could increase job satisfaction while broadening career horizons. Mentorship programs can offer guidance, advice, and access to potential career openings while creating long-lasting client relationships that can result in repeat business and positive word-of-mouth recommendations from clients.

Overall, relationships play an essential role in our personal and professional lives. By investing time and effort into developing strong bonds between ourselves and other people in our lives, we can reap the benefits that come from having an ally network at our side.

FORMING AND NURTURING STRONG RELATIONSHIPS

Establishing and nurturing strong relationships takes effort and intentionality. Here are eight techniques for creating and keeping them.

1. Exhibit genuine interest: Asking pertinent questions and actively listening with an eye toward empathy demonstrates genuine interest in another individual to build trust and strengthen connections. Doing so helps establish lasting bonds of affection between people.

2. Be genuine and authentic: Just be yourself and allow your personality to show. People will connect more with you if you remain genuine and authentic.

3. Discover common ground: Look for shared experiences or interests to deepen the bond, such as hobbies, passions, or professional ambitions.

4. Show appreciation: Express gratitude and show appreciation for another's contributions, time, and efforts by simply saying thank you or acknowledging their hard work. Doing this helps build positive and supportive relationships.

5. Communicate effectively: Effective communication is vital to any healthy relationship. Be open and honest in your communication style while actively listening to what the other person has to say, without making assumptions or jumping to conclusions.

6. Be forgiving: No one is perfect, and mistakes happen from time to time, so practicing forgiveness and letting go of grudges to foster healthy relationships is key to maintaining positive interactions and healthy interactions between people.

7. Dedicate time and effort: Maintaining strong relationships requires dedication. Be available for each other through regular check-ins or spending quality time together.

8. Be receptive to feedback: Listen carefully to feedback from others and be willing to adjust in order to enhance the relationship. Show respect for their opinion and commitment to maintaining strong bonds between you. By adopting these techniques, you can build and nurture meaningful connections personally and professionally. Take an equal part in making these connections flourishing relationships! Remember that relationships require effort from both sides for them to thrive!

SETTING BOUNDARIES AND COMMUNICATING EFFECTIVELY

Relationships can bring both joy and fulfillment; however, they can also present challenges. It is essential that boundaries be set clearly to avoid miscommunication between partners and to preserve healthy relationships. Here are eight effective strategies for setting boundaries and communicating effectively.

1. Recognize your limits: Being clear about your individual needs, values, and boundaries is key to communicating them effectively to others.

2. Communicate clearly: To effectively express your needs or boundaries, always communicate clearly using "I" statements, without placing blame or accusation on anyone.

3. Listen actively: Active listening involves focusing on understanding what lies within another's perspective, responding with empathy and understanding.

4. Acknowledging differences: Acknowledging differences of opinion, values, and perspective is vital to creating and maintaining positive and respectful relationships.

5. Address issues promptly: Address issues quickly and directly in order to prevent resentment and preserve a healthy relationship. Immediately address issues as they arise in order to avoid them becoming bigger problems, while being assertive yet respectful when communicating your concerns.

6. Employ positive language: Use positive language when communicating your needs or boundaries. Rather than saying *I do not wish for you to do this*, try saying *I would prefer that you did this*.

7. Stay consistent: Establish and adhere to boundaries consistently to avoid confusion and to build trust within a relationship.

8. Take responsibility: Accept responsibility for your own actions and mistakes instead of placing the blame elsewhere for issues or weaknesses within yourself or society as a whole.

By setting clear boundaries and communicating effectively, we can foster healthy and positive relationships in our life. Remember that healthy relationships involve mutual respect, communication, and understanding between all members involved.

Building and maintaining strong relationships requires work and intention on our part, but conflicts and misunderstandings are inevitable in any relationship. By applying the strategies and techniques outlined here, we can strengthen our bonds while managing challenging situations more gracefully and with empathy.

Relationships are an essential aspect of our lives, and investing in them can bring immense happiness, fulfillment, and support. By prioritizing communication, setting boundaries, and showing appreciation to those we care for we can form strong and long-lasting connections with those closest to us. Doing so makes personal and professional interactions easier and creates lives full of meaningful connections and lasting friendships.

Building and maintaining strong relationships are vital skills for personal and professional success. By showing genuine interest, being reliable, authentic, finding common ground, and showing appreciation, we can forge strong bonds between ourselves and other individuals.

Establishing boundaries, communicating effectively, respecting differences, and addressing issues quickly are all keys to maintaining healthy and positive relationships. Spending the time and effort building strong bonds can create more fulfilling lives.

"Relationships are the fabric of our existence, woven with threads of love, trust, and mutual respect."

Deepak Chopra

CHAPTER nine
PASSION AND PURPOSE

Chapter 9
PASSION AND PURPOSE

After much meditation and reflection, I discovered my true passions and realized I was neglecting my dreams and goals. As soon as I realized my purpose in life was to encourage others to see the good in people and be a positive influence, my motivation to write this book became apparent. My desire to inspire and be a positive influence in other people's lives sparked this passion project—writing this book—and inspired me to begin recording my thoughts and experiences. It all stemmed from a deep-seated desire for influence in this world while helping others do the same.

No matter how small our actions may seem, each person can have the power to bring about change in our world. I hope that through this book I can empower readers to recognize their own ability to make a difference and equip them with tools and motivation necessary to take action. Whether you are searching for meaning in life, ways to create positive change within your community, or simply seeking encouragement and inspiration, my hope is that this book provides you with guidance and support necessary for taking steps forward with confidence and purpose.

As soon as I started outlining my book, I knew it would give me the platform to share my experiences and insights with a broader audience. My intention was to offer practical strategies for people looking to cultivate positivity and kindness into their daily lives and spread these values throughout society. When I embarked upon this endeavor, it gave me a sense of purpose that had never before come my way. I knew this was something meant for me, and I was determined to see it through to completion.

To anyone having difficulty discovering their purpose, I advise taking some time to reflect on what brings you joy. Recall when and where in life you felt the greatest sense of fulfillment. What were you doing or with whom were you spending most of your time?

Once you have identified your passions, it's time to put them into action. Begin small by dedicating just a little time each day toward exploring them further. Volunteer, join a group, or find an advisor who can assist.

Do not fear making mistakes. Chasing after your passions and finding your purpose are an ongoing journey, and mistakes are okay as long as you keep pushing forward without giving up.

As my journey continues, the more I appreciate people for what they bring to life situations. I have realized that everyone has something positive to offer. Rather than criticizing or judging others, which often reflects insecurities about ourselves, look at the positive aspects of others. If you find yourself needing to put others down in order to feel better about yourself, take time for some inner work. Release negative feelings within yourself, and you might just find relief!

I find great joy offering authentic compliments and encouragement to those around me and witnessing their effects on their lives. I have learned the power of being a positive force in someone's life. Being a positive force can influence and encourage someone else to pursue their passions and find purposeful paths of their own.

Rise Above and Own Your Power

Anyone struggling should remember they can achieve anything they put their mind to. Rise above, own your power, and pursue your passions and purpose with intention and determination. Additionally, always see the good in others by giving compliments and encouraging whenever possible. It may just give someone else the push they need to pursue their own passions and purpose and will have an incredibly positive effect on both of your lives.

As individuals, we all possess our own unique talents, interests, and aspirations that define who we are. Pursuing our passions and finding our purpose are essential to overall happiness and fulfillment in life. Engaging in activities we find enjoyable provides a sense of joy and purpose that can positively influence other areas. In this chapter we will examine the significance of pursuing passions and discovering purpose while discussing techniques for identifying them as well as strategies for taking steps toward our goals.

PURSUING OUR PASSIONS AND FINDING OUR PURPOSE

As we pursue our passions and discover our purpose, we experience an uplifting feeling that goes far beyond external rewards such as money or recognition. When we do what brings us fulfillment and joy, the positive energy generated can positively influence all aspects of life—relationships, health, and overall well-being.

Pursuing our passions can also help us develop new skills, expand our perspectives, and open doors to personal and professional growth. Being without meaning or passion in our lives can be discouraging and leaves us feeling like there's something missing, leading us to feel lost or disconnected. Pursuing our passions and discovering our purpose can help create a life that's meaningful, aligns with our values, and brings us joy. Being enthusiastic about something makes it much more likely we put forth the time and effort required for its completion, providing increased confidence, self-esteem, and a sense of achievement along the way.

Discovering our purpose can also assist us in making wiser decisions, setting meaningful goals, and leading a happier, more satisfying lifestyle.

Pursuing our passions and discovering our purpose are two great ways to foster personal development and growth. When engaging in activities that we enjoy doing, we are more likely to learn new things and develop skills we weren't previously aware of. Similarly, when finding our purpose, we can devote energy and efforts toward activities that reflect our values and goals and help lead us toward personal development and fulfillment.

Pursuing our passions and discovering our purpose can have far-reaching repercussions for ourselves and those we care about, including relationships and communities. By participating in activities we find enjoyable, we may meet like-minded individuals with similar interests who share common values and lead to potential friendships and social connections. When we find our purpose we can use our skills, talents, and resources to create meaningful change within communities around us and provide true transformation of society at large.

Finding our passions and purpose can be challenging; however, the process requires self-reflection, exploration, and experimentation to discover what truly motivates and inspires us. But the effort will pay off, leading us to live more meaningful lives by following our dreams.

Pursuing our passions and discovering our purpose can have a tremendously positive effect on our lives, leading to personal development, fulfillment, and an enhanced sense of meaning and purpose. By engaging in activities that align with our values and goals, we can build a life that brings us joy while making an impactful contribution to society at large.

IDENTIFYING OUR PASSIONS AND PURPOSE

Identifying our passions and purpose can be a challenging process, it requires introspection and self-reflection. But there are techniques we can use to gain clarity into what truly motivates us.

Reflection can be an effective strategy to uncover our passions and purposes. Reflecting upon past experiences can reveal activities that brought the most happiness and fulfillment, helping us discover themes or patterns that might point us in the right direction.

Here are four techniques to help you discover your passions and purposes.

1. Consider what brings you joy: Take time to consider which activities bring the most pleasure and fulfillment for you, whether in free-time activities that help pass time or activities that get your mind off work and keep things interesting—or both!

2. Evaluate your values: Values serve as guides for our decisions and actions, so identifying your core values and considering how they align with current activities and goals are an integral step toward fulfilling them.

3. Understand your unique assets: Take time to identify and understand your unique skill set and talents, such as what you are good at or things people have praised you about.

4. Visualize your ideal life: Take time to imagine your ideal life and what activities or priorities and goals it may entail.

An alternative strategy is to explore new activities and experiences. Opening ourselves up to different experiences may help us discover hidden passions or interests we hadn't considered previously. Seeking feedback from others may provide invaluable insight into our own strengths and talents.

These five techniques may assist in discovering your passions and purposes.

1. Keep a journal: Writing can be a powerful way of self-reflection and introspection. Take time each day to reflect upon your experiences and emotions, considering which activities or experiences provide the greatest joy or fulfillment, and which actions leave you feeling depleted or disillusioned. Over time, patterns may emerge that reveal your passions and purpose in life.

2. Take a personality test: Many personality tests are available online, and these exams can provide valuable insight into your strengths, values, and interests. Myers–Briggs Type Indicator (MBTI) or StrengthsFinder tests offer great ways of discovering natural tendencies or preferences that could point you toward possible career paths or hobbies that align with your passions and purposes.

3. Seek mentors: Mentors can be invaluable allies as you discover your passions and purpose in life. Seek individuals with experience in areas that interest you who can provide advice and feedback throughout your journey. Joining professional organizations or networking groups may also provide the chance to meet potential mentors.

4. Volunteer: Volunteering can be an incredible way to uncover your passions and purpose while giving back to your community. Seek volunteer opportunities that appeal to you, while being open-minded about trying something new. Volunteering also serves as a great opportunity to gain new skills that could boost your resume.

5. Employ mindfulness techniques: Mindfulness techniques like meditation or yoga can be effective tools for clearing away clutter in the mind and clarifying goals and aspirations.

Take time each day to practice mindfulness and reflect. Writing down or journaling about what truly inspires and motivates you can provide invaluable clarity into who inspires and drives you. Identifying passions and purpose requires patience, self-reflection, and an openness to new experiences. By using these techniques you may gain clarity into what truly moves and motivates you.

TAKING STEPS TOWARD ACHIEVING YOUR GOALS

Once you've identified our passions and purposes, the next step should be taking steps toward achieving your goals. One effective strategy would be breaking them down into smaller, more manageable tasks to help keep you focused, motivated, and progress toward them.

Associating ourselves with supportive people who share our values and beliefs is also crucial, helping us remain motivated, accountable and gain invaluable feedback and support.

Here are four effective strategies that will help you take immediate action.

1. Establish specific and measurable goals: Define your goals as specific and measurable to stay motivated and track progress effectively. Having this clear road map can help keep you on the right path to achieving them.

2. Draft an action plan: Make an action plan to meet your goals. Identify all of the necessary steps and resources required.

3. Stay motivated: Stay inspired and focused by remembering why you started in the first place, celebrating successes as they come and learning from failures.

4. Surround yourself with positive people: Find encouragement from friends, family, mentors, or coaches that can provide invaluable guidance along your journey.

Pursuing your passions and finding your purpose are both essential elements of happiness and fulfillment. By using techniques to identify them and strategies to take steps toward fulfilling them, we can craft meaningful lives that align with our values while giving us great joy. Don't give up; the journey to finding our passions and purposes can never end. Don't delay taking steps toward realizing them now!

Strategizing ways to achieve our goals can help us take meaningful steps toward leading more fulfilling lives. Breaking goals down into smaller tasks, surrounding ourselves with supportive people, and cultivating a growth mindset are all effective strategies that can keep us focused and on track toward meeting our goals.

Remind yourself that achieving your goals isn't always a linear process, with setbacks and failures inevitable along the way. By welcoming challenges as opportunities for personal growth and learning, you can stay motivated while moving toward your goals more quickly.

Success lies in remaining committed and taking continuous steps toward what matters to you most.

"Passion is the fire that ignites your purpose, propelling you to make a meaningful difference in the world."

Tony Robbins

CHAPTER *ten*
REFLECTIONS ON THE JOURNEY

Chapter 10
REFLECTIONS ON THE JOURNEY

As I reflect on my life using techniques outline in this book, I slowly began to recognize a strength within myself that I never realized was there. Looking back over my journey and my experiences that had formed me into who I am today, it became clear that I had always been capable of rising above challenges and owning my power. Yet somehow I had never fully acknowledged or accepted this ability.

As I worked through the process of rebuilding my inner strength, confidence, and self-worth, I found that my sense of empowerment increased considerably. I began making decisions that were right for me even if they weren't always easy. Trusting myself and my instincts, realizing my value, and aligning with my true sense of self brought immense happiness! Although this process will never stop being work in progress, it brings me great satisfaction knowing who I am becoming as I go along!

Life was not always smooth sailing for me. At times I fell off track, but I kept pushing forward, reminding myself that I could handle whatever life threw my way.

Now, as I reflect on my journey, I feel immensely proud of what I've accomplished. I know that I am strong, capable, and deserving of happiness—and want others to know this too. Never allow anyone tell you otherwise. Never believe you cannot do something you want to achieve!

Now that you've reached the end of this book, I hope that you have gained insight into reclaiming your inner strength, confidence, and self-worth. Over the course of its chapters, I shared various strategies and techniques designed to combat negative self-talk while building positive self-images. We discussed setting realistic goals, practicing self-care techniques, and surrounding yourself with positive influences as ways of improving mental wellness.

Remember that rebuilding inner strength, confidence, and self-worth is a journey that takes consistent effort and dedication to achieve success. Although obstacles may arise along your journey, it's vital that you remain positive by trusting in yourself and never giving up your goals!

UNLOCK YOUR INNER STRENGTH, CONFIDENCE, AND SEL-WORTH

Take time to appreciate how far you have come on your journey so far, celebrating every victory however small or insignificant each may seem. Remember, each step forward brings you one step closer to reaching your goal.

Recognizing and appreciating all of the challenges and obstacles you have overcome along the way can also be very valuable, offering invaluable lessons while aiding growth and strengthening resilience. See these challenges as opportunities to gain useful experience and build strength within yourself.

REGAINING INNER STRENGTH, CONFIDENCE, AND SELF-WORTH

As you embark on your journey, remember that you are not alone. There are thousands of others working hard to regain their inner strength, confidence, and sense of worthiness as well. Don't hesitate to seek assistance from family, friends, or professionals should assistance be required; seeking support shows strength not weakness.

I encourage you to continue standing tall and owning your power. You deserve love and respect, and should feel empowered within yourself. Stay committed to your goals, never forgetting that only *you* have the ability to create the life that's perfect for you.

Remember, building inner strength, confidence, and self-worth requires not just one act but is an ongoing journey. There may be setbacks and difficulties along the way. What matters is staying committed to your personal growth and development.

One key strategy for maintaining a positive self-image is practicing self-compassion. This means treating yourself with kindness and understanding just as you would treat a close friend. When you make mistakes or encounter setbacks, try offering yourself encouragement and support rather than harsh self-criticism.

Focusing on your strengths and accomplishments is another effective strategy to boost self-esteem. While it may be easy to fall into negative self-talk and dwell on failures and weaknesses, this can damage your sense of self-worth. So it is wiser to regularly reflect upon all the good that has come your way and be proud of them all, no matter how small the successes may appear.

Maintaining a positive self-image requires surrounding yourself with positive influences, including spending time with supportive friends and family members, seeking positive role models, or joining supportive communities or groups.

Regaining your inner strength, confidence, and self-worth can be a long and arduous journey that requires honesty, self-reflection, and the willingness to challenge negative beliefs and behaviors. But with dedication and persistence it is possible to establish positive self-images that help lead to fulfilling lives.

As you embark on your journey toward rebuilding inner strength, confidence, and self-worth, remember it will require ongoing effort and commitment from you. Though there will likely be moments of discouragement or frustration along the way, remain dedicated to your goals by staying committed to them rather than giving up on yourself.

Recognize that setbacks and challenges are part of life. Nobody's perfect, and everyone makes mistakes or faces setbacks at some point in their life. The key is approaching these challenges with an open mindset and viewing them as opportunities to learn rather than seeing them as failures.

One effective strategy to stay motivated and committed to personal development is setting realistic goals. Your goals should be specific, measurable, attainable, and divided into manageable steps. This way, setting ambitious yet attainable targets can help build confidence as you make strides toward reaching larger objectives.

Practice self-care to promote your mental and emotional well-being. This may involve engaging in regular exercise, sleeping enough hours each night, practicing mindfulness meditation or other mindfulness practices, or seeking professional counseling when necessary. By caring for yourself you can build resilience against stressors and overcome challenges more easily.

Reclaiming your inner strength, confidence, and self-worth is a deeply personal journey, with different results for everyone. Stay committed to the process by practicing self-compassion and surrounding yourself with positive influences. By doing this, you can build a positive self-image while living an enriching and meaningful life.

FINAL THOUGHTS AND ENCOURAGEMENT

Take time to celebrate all of your successes on this journey toward finding inner strength, confidence, and self-worth. Celebrating even small wins can help build momentum and remain motivating as you continue along your path to reclaiming them.

Be mindful of the challenges and obstacles you have overcome throughout your journey, for they have taught you invaluable lessons and made you stronger and more resilient. By acknowledging and using them as opportunities to gain experience and grow, you can develop resilience and confidence that allows you to overcome adversity with ease.

Rise Above and Own Your Power

Be patient and kind to yourself as you continue on your journey, keeping in mind that personal development is an ongoing process, and that progress may not always be linear. There may be times when you feel stuck or discouraged, but stay committed to your goals. Don't give up!

Reclaiming your inner strength, confidence, and self-worth is an intimate journey that takes much effort and dedication. But with perseverance and an openness to learn new things it is possible to build a positive self-image and live a meaningful and satisfying life.

Reclaiming inner strength, confidence, and self-worth may seem an uphill battle at times, but you are not alone, and it is perfectly okay if you make mistakes along the way. Accept your power and worth without feeling shamed into staying quiet. Embrace what life has brought your way with an eye toward living a fulfilling and happy life. Don't shy away from owning up to who you really are. Don't forget you are strong and can achieve any goal that lies before you.

This book was designed to give you tools and motivation to rebuild your inner strength, self-worth, and confidence. Remember that great achievements can be accomplished. Your worth does not depend on external influences. Stay shining, grow stronger, and believe in yourself!

"Owning your story and loving yourself through that process is the bravest thing that you will ever do."

Brené Brown

ACKNOWLEDGMENTS

My dear friends and family,

Thank you so much for being there for me during my most trying period in my life. Your continued support and encouragement have enabled me to overcome even the toughest obstacles, making the journey through each difficult day that much easier. I truly consider myself blessed to count you among my friends.

Life was throwing me curveballs, and I didn't know how to cope. Your love and support provided me strength to carry on. You reminded me that I am loved, valued, and appreciated even when I couldn't see if for myself. Your thoughtful words and acts of kindness gave me hope and renewed my faith in humanity. Thank you.

Thank you to each and every one of you for having had such an influence in my life. I feel blessed to call each and every one of you my friends and family. Thank you for always being there when I needed someone the most, reminding me I am never alone.

ABOUT THE AUTHOR

Lizaida Alvarez is a manager in the healthcare sector, a real estate professional, a certified life coach, an entrepreneur, and now an author.

Lizaida was born and raised in Puerto Rico. She grew up in a small town, fueled by her dreams and aspirations. Even after leaving her roots behind to move to the United States at fourteen years old, she remained hopeful for a better future. Despite coming from humble beginnings, not knowing English, and starting a family at an incredibly young age, she knew she had something more in her and was determined to fulfill her dreams and aspirations.

Throughout her life she has faced many difficulties, including a divorce after twenty years of marriage, which left her emotionally and financially drained. She refused to let these challenges define her, and instead she took charge of her life and rose above them. In this book, she shares her journey and the techniques she used to overcome the most difficult part of it. She believes that no matter what brings you down, you have the power within you to rise above, rewrite your story, and create a fulfilling life.

In her pursuit of personal and professional development, she has navigated her own path of learning and growth. Engaging in personal development masterclass, workshops, reading and research, she has gained a profound understanding of human behavior and developed a passion for empowering others to see their full potential. Her journey is a testament to the transformative power of continuous learning, resilience, and the belief in the ability to create positive change, both within ourselves and in the lives of others.

Visit lizaidaalvarez.com.

Follow Lizaida on Instagram @lizaida.alvarez

Rise Above and Own Your Power

NOTES

NOTES

NOTES

NOTES

NOTES

NOTES

NOTES

www.ingramcontent.com/pod-product-compliance
Lightning Source LLC
Chambersburg PA
CBHW050634160426
43194CB00010B/1667